ELEGY FOR MIPPY II
FOR TROMBONE ALONE

BY

LEONARD BERNSTEIN

LEONARD
BERNSTEIN
Music Publishing
Company LLC

BOOSEY & HAWKES

DISTRIBUTED BY
HAL•LEONARD®

For my brother Burtie

Elegy for Mippy II*

for Trombone alone

Trombone*

Leonard Bernstein

*Mippy II was a mongrel belonging to my brother Burtie.

**The trombonist should accompany himself by tapping one foot, *mf*, four to the bar, e.g.

BTB-15

U.S. $10.99

M-060-07139-3

HL48010873

ISBN-13: 978-1-4950-1661-5

Distributed By

HAL LEONARD

48010873

BOOSEY & HAWKES

DISTRIBUTED BY

HAL•LEONARD®